TAKING

THE NEXT STEP

From Not Being Able to Walk to Walking

with the Power of My Words

BY: ALBERT KIRKLAND

Taking the Next Step, From not being able to Walk to Walking with the Power of my Words
Copyright ©2023 Albert Kirkland

Printed in United States of America

First printing, 2023

Library of Congress Registration Number: TXu2385066

ISBN: 979-8-9891723-1-3

DEDICATION

This book is dedicated to my father, daughter, and son: Albert Kirkland Senior, Nevaeh Kirkland, and Albert Kirkland III.

Contents

INTRODUCTION

May this book shower blessings upon the reader, filling their heart with love, enriching their mind with knowledge, and guiding them with wisdom. Let the one who reads this book be a beacon of light, sharing its profound wisdom with all those in need. *Taking the Next Step* is the gentle nudge that propels us forward on our unique paths. Embrace the journey toward becoming the best version of yourself, for in that pursuit lies true happiness. Remember, the divine resides within each and every one of us, guiding us toward our purpose and showering us with abundant blessings.

The purpose of this book is to ignite a fire within you, inspiring and motivating you to embark on the next chapter of your life's journey. Let's kick-start this incredible journey with empowering words for you, dear reader:

Believe in yourself, for you possess everything necessary to take that leap forward. Embrace your thoughts and dreams and become a master of your own destiny! True transformation begins with an honest self-assessment, acknowledging your flaws, and embracing the desire for change without placing blame, not even on yourself. As you transform, your future will undergo a magnificent metamorphosis. Remember, as children of the divine, lack and want hold no power over us, for we are connected to abundance itself. The greatest power lies within you, capable of surmounting any adversity, conquering doubts, and turning your long-cherished dreams into reality. Taking the Next Step is the catalyst that will guide you from the shadows of darkness into the radiant light of your own greatness. Let the wise words of Lao Tzu resonate: "A journey of a thousand miles must begin with a single step."

CHAPTER 1: JUST STARTING

SOME ENCOURAGING WORDS TO THE READER:

Let us embark on a journey of transformation, beginning each day with renewed vigor and positivity. It's time to nourish our bodies with healthier choices, to move and exercise, and to truly embrace the gift of life. Let's break free from the clutches of negativity and immerse ourselves in a world of optimism and possibility. Speak uplifting words, walk with confidence, and radiate positivity in all that we do. Embrace the power of the present moment, for it holds the key to unlocking our fullest potential. By emptying ourselves, we create space to receive more, to learn, and to connect with the depths of our being. Together, let us unite and work harmoniously, forging a better world and a brighter future for our children. It all starts with that first step, igniting the flame of change, embarking on a journey of personal growth, and reshaping the course of our lives. Remember, in the act of beginning, we unlock the door to the divine presence within ourselves. Let us embrace this journey of transformation and embrace the limitless possibilities that lie ahead.

WHAT IS JUST STARTING:

Just starting is one of our most powerful and important traits. Just starting is the act of taking the initiative and mustering the courage to begin, even when doubts and obstacles loom large. It's a challenging step for many, as they may believe they lack the necessary resources or abilities to embark on the journey. However, a shift in perspective can make all the difference. Viewing the next step as a series of small stepping stones rather than daunting leaps can make getting started easier. It starts with believing that you already possess within you all that you need to begin. This belief empowers you to overcome any hesitation or self-doubt. The power to choose to start resides within each of us, and it is the essential foundation for embarking on the next step. When you recognize and embrace this power, there is no room for lack or doubt to hinder your progress. Remember, just starting is a choice, and it's a choice you have the ability to control. By initiating the next step, you tap into the inherent strength and potential that lies within you.

HOW CAN JUST STARTING BENEFIT ANYONE?

Just starting has the power to help anyone overcome their difficulties in life. The journey of starting varies for each individual, as we all have unique circumstances and challenges to navigate. That's why it's important not to compare ourselves to others or their situations when taking that first step. Instead, we must turn inward, focusing on our own healing and personal growth. By initiating the process of self-improvement, we set the stage for progress and transformation. Just starting signifies a commitment to our own well-being and the betterment of our lives. This commitment, in turn, fuels motivation, happiness, and confidence. It enables us to identify areas in need of improvement and develop a clear plan to achieve our goals. Through the power of just starting, we empower ourselves to embrace personal progress and embark on a journey of self-discovery and fulfillment.

The benefits of just starting are numerous and profound. When we take that initial step, we begin to believe in something greater than ourselves. This belief can lead to the development of faith as our conviction and commitment to that belief deepen over time. As we gather more knowledge and gain experience, we may start to witness evidence that supports our belief, further strengthening courage, acceptance, and happiness in our lives. Through the power of just starting, we can embark on a transformative journey that leads us to a place of unwavering faith, bringing us fulfillment, resilience, and a profound sense of purpose.

MY LIFE EXPERIENCE:

As I reflect on my journey, I ponder the pivotal moment that propelled me to begin the process of self-improvement and prioritize my well-being. To offer an illustrative example to my readers, I will share an event from my own life that necessitated the undertaking of numerous steps. Initially, I found myself adrift, unsure of the path to embark upon first. Taking that initial step proved to be immensely challenging at that juncture. However, a significant realization dawned upon me—I possessed the power of just starting, a realization that ultimately shaped the person I have become today.

July 5, 2010, marked a fateful day that forever altered the course of my existence. It was on that dreadful day that I fell victim to a senseless act of violence, mercilessly shot multiple times by an assailant whose identity remains shrouded in mystery. That day, at that given moment, I ceased to exist. The motives behind this heinous act, even to this day, elude me, leaving me grappling with unanswered questions and an overwhelming sense of bewilderment. The aftermath of that traumatic incident left me confined to a wheelchair—my body paralyzed from the waist down, and my spirit shattered by the enigma of who and why.

The impact of this drastic change in my life unleashed a torrent of negative and unhealthy emotions that engulfed my being. From once possessing logical reasoning, providing for my children, and embracing life with an open mind, I now found myself submerged in a dark abyss of despair. Hatred toward the world consumed my thoughts, the trauma etching deep scars within my psyche. The weight of profound depression pressed upon me, suffocating any glimmer of hope. Anxiety gnawed at my every waking moment, a constant companion in my battle to make sense of this tragedy.

Not only did I suffer physically and mentally, but I also endured the heart-wrenching loss of friends and family members who, in the face of my adversity, gradually withdrew from my life. The pain of their absence compounded my anguish, leaving me to navigate the depths of despair with weakening support. The reality of my newfound disability became an unyielding source of grief, an insurmountable barrier preventing me from ever walking again, forever stripping away a fundamental aspect of my identity.

Within the confines of these harrowing circumstances, I found myself trapped, unable to muster the strength or will to take that crucial first step toward healing and personal growth. The weight of my experiences kept me locked in a cycle of stagnation, preventing me from unleashing my true potential and embracing the best version of my life that lay dormant within.

But amidst the darkness, a flicker of resilience began to emerge—a glimmer of light that whispered the possibility of transformation. I realized that although the trauma and pain were real, I still held the power to shape my own destiny. With every ounce of courage I could summon, I mustered the strength to defy the despair and take the first hesitant steps toward reclaiming my life. The journey ahead would be arduous, but the mere act of starting became an act of defiance—a proclamation that I would not be defined solely by the tragedy that befell me.

In the face of immense adversity, I embarked on a path of self-discovery, one that demanded unyielding determination and unwavering resilience. It was through this process of healing and growth that I began to realize the incredible strength that resided within me. As I gradually shed the shackles of self-pity and despair, I discovered the capacity to rebuild, to find purpose and meaning in the face of unimaginable hardship.

While the scars of that day may never fully fade, I stand here today as a testament to the indomitable human spirit. The journey of self-improvement and personal transformation continues, and I am committed to embracing each step with unwavering determination. Through the darkness and the pain, I am determined to forge a life that surpasses the limitations that were imposed upon me. My journey serves as a reminder that even in the depths of despair, the power to rise above, to just start, resides within us all.

HOW JUST STARTING LED ME TO MY NEXT STEP:

These struggles I faced became the catalyst for me to seize the initiative in pursuit of a better version of myself. Determined to transcend my difficulties, I embarked on a quest to discover my next step—the pivotal moment that would set me on a transformative journey toward overcoming my challenges. It was during this profound exploration that I found power in the embrace of faith, which became the guiding force propelling me forward.

CHAPTER 2: FAITH

SOME ENCOURAGING WORDS FOR THE READER:

Embrace the next step with unwavering faith as you embark on the journey of self-education. Allow faith to infuse every aspect of your life, illuminating your perspective and transforming your outlook. Release doubts and embrace the belief in what can be, letting go of the limitations of what isn't.

With faith as your steadfast companion, embrace moments of silence and introspection, trusting that God is diligently rebuilding you from within. Believe in the power of your dreams and have the courage to conquer your goals. Recognize that within you lies the innate potential and resources needed for personal growth and self-improvement. Let faith be more than a mere step; it is the key that unlocks the door to the divine presence within you. Embrace the next step with unwavering faith, for it holds the promise of a life transformed and a connection to the boundless grace that surrounds you.

The next question that arose within me was, "How can I persevere and continue taking the next step amidst the challenges I face?"

The answer was beautifully simple: faith. To truly progress and evolve, it is crucial to cultivate trust and unwavering belief in oneself. The nature of faith required to navigate life's journey may differ from person to person, shaped by individual beliefs and unique circumstances.

First, fostering a deep-rooted belief in one's own abilities and potential is absolute. By acknowledging and valuing your inherent strengths, you pave the way for remarkable growth. Second, placing trust in the universe or a higher power grants knowledge and guidance, lending you the courage to forge ahead, even when faced with uncertainty. Embracing risk-taking and embracing the unknown with an open heart and mind are further hallmarks of faith's transformative power.

To continue progressing, it is vital to release fear and doubt, cultivating a positive mindset that illuminates every facet of life. By embracing the profound essence of faith, you embark on a profound journey of self-discovery, unearthing the vast reservoirs of potential within you. Faith propels you forward, endowing you with the confidence, purpose, and resilience needed to pursue your dreams and aspirations. With faith as your steadfast companion, you will unlock the abundance that dwells within, embracing a life of fulfillment and endless possibilities.

WHAT IS FAITH?

Faith can be understood as a deep trust or unwavering confidence in something greater than oneself beyond the realm of ordinary perception. It transcends mere belief and extends into a profound inner knowing or realization. Faith is not dependent on external validation or proof but arises from a direct experience of the interconnectedness of all things or the inherent wisdom of the universe. It is an intuitive understanding that surpasses intellectual understanding and is grounded in a profound spiritual awareness. It acknowledges the limitations of conceptual knowledge and embraces the mysteries of life with an open heart and mind.

Faith can provide individuals with a sense of purpose, guidance, and inner stability. It serves as a guiding light during times of uncertainty and challenges, allowing individuals to navigate life with greater equanimity and resilience. It fosters a deep sense of love and compassion for all beings, recognizing the inherent unity and sacredness of existence. It may manifest differently for each individual based on their unique spiritual journey and insights.

HOW CAN HAVING FAITH BENEFIT ANYONE?

Taking the next step toward faith can bring a sense of purpose, hope, and guidance to one's life. It can provide a support system of like-minded individuals who share similar beliefs and values. Faith can also offer comfort during difficult times and serve as a source of inspiration for personal growth and development. Additionally, faith can improve mental health and well-being through practices such as mindfulness, gratitude, and forgiveness. Exploring and deepening one's faith can lead to a greater sense of fulfillment and meaning in life. Ultimately, the benefits of faith lie in its ability to provide a sense of inner peace, guidance, purpose, resilience, and a deeper connection to oneself and others.

MY LIFE EXPERIENCE:

For my cherished readers, I humbly share a profound chapter of my life that tested the very fabric of my faith. It was a time cloaked in the depths of a dark and relentless depression, where every breath seemed to weigh upon my weary soul. In the face of such desolation, I found myself consumed by feelings of worthlessness, both as a man and as a father to my precious children. Many nights of crying, many nights of loneliness, and many times I wanted to give up. The world around me appeared devoid of light, its vibrant hues replaced by a black canvas of despair.

I vividly recall my daughter, then just four years old, clasping my hand with her tiny fingers, her innocent voice resonating with unwavering hope, "Daddy, walk! Get up, Daddy; you can walk!" Each tender plea struck my heart like an arrow, piercing the depths of my being. The loss of my ability to walk had become a cavernous void that echoed with haunting negativity. As the ancient proverb goes, "As a man thinketh, so shall he become," and indeed, my thoughts mirrored the darkness that enveloped me.

In those moments, as I descended into the abyss where even the most caring souls could not reach me, where the walls closed in with an oppressive weight, and where the chilling embrace of despair crept closer, a voice, barely a whisper, emerged from the shadows. It was a voice that possessed an unshakable confidence, a resolute calmness that defied the surrounding chaos. It proclaimed, "You are the Will of God! Yes, you have stumbled and fallen; yes, you have tasted the bitterness of defeat; and yes, you stand alone now. But what you are not, my child, is defeated.

"All that you have lost shall be reclaimed," the voice assured me. "For in every failure lies a profound lesson, and through your brokenness, you shall rise like a phoenix from the ashes. I have stripped away your desires to reveal the essence of your true needs. Those who have departed from your life were never meant to walk alongside you. Though you may not walk with your legs, you possess the extraordinary power to walk with your words. When darkness engulfs your spirit, know that I am forever present within you. I shall never forsake you, for you are my beloved child. You possess the indomitable Will of God, capable of overcoming any adversity that may cross your path."

This ethereal voice, this beacon of hope that resonated within, became the catalyst for my journey into faith. With each passing day, I embraced these thoughts, allowing them to seep into the depths of my being. They transformed from mere words to an unwavering belief, infusing me with newfound strength and resilience. In realizing the profound truth that I held the Will of God within me, I took the next step toward a life illuminated by faith.

How did faith lead me to my next step of having courage?

Faith served as the catalyst that propelled me toward the next step of courage in my life's journey. With an unwavering belief in a higher power, I found profound meaning in every action and realized that I wasn't alone. In the face of adversity, faith became my unwavering companion, offering guidance and infusing me with hope when the path seemed impossible to travel. Guided by faith, I summoned the strength to navigate treacherous terrain and endure hardships that tested my own faith. The knowledge that a higher power watched over me empowered me to confront each obstacle head-on, refusing to succumb to doubt or fear. Embracing faith ignited a boldness within me, propelling me to act in alignment with my deepest beliefs and values. With faith as my guiding light, I embraced risks, ventured into the unknown, and faced challenges with unwavering determination. It was through this courageous stance, fortified by faith, that I discovered the true extent of my capabilities and embraced the person I was destined to become.

CHAPTER 3: COURAGE

Embrace the power of courage as you embark on your extraordinary journey, allowing its guiding light to lead you toward a profound transformation of self-care, self-love, and authenticity. Summon your inner courage to construct a foundation of unwavering confidence, strengthening your belief in your limitless abilities and untapped potential. Embrace the force of consistency and solitude as opportunities to rediscover yourself, unearthing newfound strength and resilience. Seize the reins of your life with courage, reclaiming control over your destiny and fearlessly confronting your deepest fears. Release the shackles of doubt and uncertainty, embracing courage as the divine key that unlocks your inner strength and unbreakable connection to the essence within. Believe in your boundless capacity to soar beyond limitations, manifesting the magnificent life you envision. With each step forward, your boldness grows, and the world eagerly embraces the brilliance that resides within you. Embrace the power of courage as the catalyst propelling you toward greatness, unleashing your extraordinary potential.

WHAT IS COURAGE:

Courage is the quality or ability to face and overcome fear and adversity. It is the willingness to take risks, confront difficult situations, and pursue goals despite potential obstacles or uncertainty. Courage involves acting in the face of fear or discomfort, demonstrating resilience, and standing up for what one believes in, even when it may be unpopular or difficult. It often involves a sense of bravery, determination, and the willingness to step outside of one's comfort zone in pursuit of personal growth, justice, or the greater good. Courage can manifest in different forms, whether it's physical courage in facing danger, moral courage in standing up for ethical principles, or emotional courage in addressing personal vulnerabilities. It is an admirable and essential virtue that empowers individuals to overcome challenges and make a positive impact in their lives and the lives of others.

HOW CAN COURAGE BENEFIT ANYONE?

Having courage is important in life because it allows you to face your fears, take risks, and overcome challenges. It can also lead to personal growth, increased confidence, and the ability to pursue your goals and dreams. Taking the next step toward courage can benefit someone in many ways. It can help them overcome fear and doubt, build self-confidence, and improve their mental and emotional well-being. By facing their fears and taking action, they can develop resilience and become more adaptable to new challenges. This can lead to personal growth, increased success and satisfaction in life, and improved relationships with others. Courage can inspire others and create a positive impact in the world. Courage can have a trickle-down effect from parents to children. Giving children more courage will allow their self-esteem to grow and flourish. Overall, taking the next step toward courage can lead to a happier, more fulfilling life.

MY LIFE EXAMPLE:

In the depths of my life's story lies a chapter that epitomizes the struggle and triumph of the human spirit. It was a time when courage became my lifeline, as I found myself trapped in the clutches of a weakened will and relentless darkness. The weight of my circumstances threatened to consume me, leaving me immobilized in the face of a daunting reality.

In that pivotal moment, I yearned for the courage to break free from the chains of negativity and despair. As the wheelchair became my constant companion, I wrestled with the limitations imposed upon me, unable to see beyond the boundaries of my physical condition. It was within these confines that I needed the unwavering strength to transform my perspective and shift my focus to the boundless possibilities that still lay within my reach.

Summoning courage, I embarked on a journey of self-discovery and self-acceptance. It was a tumultuous battle against the negative thoughts that whispered doubt and self-deprecation into my ears. But with determination, I rose above those voices, daring to believe in my own worth and potential. I found the courage to silence the echoes of the past and embrace a new narrative, one brimming with resilience, hope, and possibility.

Courage guided me to confront my inner demons, to shed the layers of self-doubt and insecurity that had consumed me for far too long. It pushed me to challenge the preconceived notions of what I could or couldn't do, igniting a fire within me to push beyond my perceived limitations. With each passing day, I relearned how to live, not merely surviving but thriving amidst adversity.

The journey toward acceptance was the ultimate test of my courage. It required me to face the truth of my situation head-on, to confront the stark realities of my new reality with bravery. I had to find the courage to accept myself wholly and unconditionally, embracing both my strengths and vulnerabilities as essential parts of my being. In doing so, I discovered the power and beauty of self-acceptance, an anchor that grounded me amidst the storm.

But the triumph of courage did not end with self-acceptance alone. It propelled me to expand my horizons, open my mind to new possibilities, and extend compassion and understanding to others. With newfound empathy, I connected with a world that was waiting to be explored, finding solace and inspiration in the shared journeys of others.

My story is a testament to the indomitable spirit that resides within each of us. It is a reminder that even in the darkest of times, courage can serve as a guiding light, illuminating the path toward self-discovery, growth, and acceptance. Through determination and belief in our own potential, we can rise above the challenges that beset us and transform our lives into a symphony of resilience and triumph.

HOW COURAGE LED ME TO MY NEXT STEP OF FINDING ACCEPTANCE:

Obtaining courage propelled me toward the pivotal next step of acceptance in my life. It emboldened me to confront fears and uncertainties head-on, unlocking newfound self-assurance and inner strength. With courage as my ally, I embraced challenges as opportunities for growth, leading me on a profound journey of self-acceptance. Fearlessly exploring the depths of my being, I discovered the beauty in embracing every aspect of myself—the strengths, flaws, and complexities that make me unique. Courage enabled me to shed self-doubt and criticism, fostering deep self-love and appreciation. It cultivated empathy and compassion, allowing me to let go of judgment and embrace understanding. Guided by courage, acceptance became the key to unlocking a world of self-discovery, connection, and profound transformation.

CHAPTER 4: ACCEPTANCE

SOME ENCOURAGING WORDS TO THE READER:

Embrace the power of acceptance, for within it lies the key to unlocking the boundless potential that resides within you. It is not a passive surrender but rather a courageous act of embracing your true self. Acceptance is about acknowledging and embracing every part of your being—the flaws, the appearance, the past, and the present. In the realm of acceptance, there is liberation from the shackles of self-doubt and judgment. Embrace who you are, celebrate your uniqueness, and honor the experiences that have shaped you. Embracing acceptance means embracing your weaknesses as stepping stones to growth. Know that you are not defined by your shortcomings but by your unwavering spirit and the potential that lies within you.

Open your heart to the vibrant connection of all beings and invite harmony and compassion into your life. Acceptance is a catalyst for a future filled with limitless possibilities. It invites you to step into your authentic self, cultivating resilience and courage to forge your path. Trust in the divine unfolding of your life and let acceptance guide you toward a profound connection with the God within. With acceptance as your guiding principle, embark on a transformative journey of self-discovery, authenticity, and growth. Watch as it unlocks the doors to a life filled with purpose, joy, and limitless potential.

WHAT IS ACCEPTANCE?

Acceptance can be understood as a state of being in which one fully embraces and acknowledges the present moment, including oneself and the circumstances as they are, without resistance or judgment. It involves a deep surrender to the reality of the present, free from the attachment to desired outcomes or the aversion to unwanted experiences.

It arises from a place of deep wisdom and understanding that everything in life is impermanent and interconnected. It is a recognition that resistance and clinging to expectations only create suffering and perpetuate a sense of separation from the inherent wholeness of existence.

In this state of acceptance, there is a profound openness and receptivity to whatever arises, whether it be joy, pain, success, or failure. It involves an unconditional embrace of all experiences and emotions without labeling them as good or bad. It allows for deep integration of the present moment, enabling individuals to engage with life authentically and compassionately.

HOW CAN ANYONE BENEFIT FROM HAVING ACCEPTANCE?

Through acceptance, individuals can find profound peace, inner freedom, and liberation from the struggles caused by resistance and attachment. It enables them to cultivate a deep sense of compassion and interconnectedness with all of life. It is a transformative state that brings about a profound shift in perception and allows individuals to experience the profound beauty and sacredness of the present moment.

Acceptance of oneself can benefit a person in many ways. It can improve self-esteem, reduce anxiety and stress, increase happiness and life satisfaction, and lead to stronger relationships with others. When a person accepts themselves for who they are, flaws and all, they can feel more confident in their abilities and choices. They are less likely to compare themselves to others and feel inadequate. This can lead to better mental health and a more positive outlook on life. Acceptance of oneself can also lead to healthier relationships with others, as the person is more likely to be authentic and true to themselves. Overall, accepting oneself is an important step toward personal growth and a happier, more fulfilling life.

MY LIFE EXPERIENCE:

To my readers, I want to take you on a deeply personal journey of triumph over adversity and the transformative power of acceptance. There was a time in my life when the need for acceptance loomed large, and I emerged from the depths of despair to find strength in embracing my reality.

It required immense courage to embark on this path of acceptance as I grappled with the stark realization that I would never walk again. Waves of sadness and grief crashed upon me, threatening to engulf my spirit. Acceptance beckoned me, urging me to confront the profound loss I had experienced and make peace with the limitations imposed upon me.

Acceptance demanded that I confront the harsh truth that the familiar rhythms of everyday life with my children would forever be altered. I had to reconcile with the fact that I could no longer engage in physical activities with them as I once had, and the weight of this realization pressed heavily upon my heart.

Yet, amidst the darkness, I found a glimmer of hope—a beacon of triumph awaiting me on the other side of acceptance. With every ounce of strength I possessed, I took a courageous step forward, embracing the reality of my situation. I chose to accept that walking was no longer a part of my physical journey, but it would not define the essence of who I am.

In the process of accepting my limitations, I discovered newfound depths of resilience and adaptability. I learned to focus on the boundless possibilities that lay within my grasp rather than fixating on what was beyond my reach. With acceptance came the liberation to redefine my identity and embrace the unique gifts I had to offer the world.

Acceptance also entailed acknowledging the pain of my past, the relationships fractured by my own insecurities and struggles. The acceptance of my role in these fractures opened the door to healing and reconciliation. It was a humbling experience to confront the consequences of my actions, but in doing so, I discovered the power of forgiveness and the opportunity for growth and connection.

Through the prism of acceptance, I witnessed the profound beauty of life unfolding before me. It enabled me to cherish the precious moments with my children, to be fully present in their lives despite my physical limitations. I realized that our bond transcended the realm of physical activities, and our love was steadfast and unwavering.

The journey toward acceptance was arduous and fraught with pain, but it also became the crucible in which my spirit was tempered and strengthened. It taught me that acceptance is not a passive surrender but an active choice to embrace life's circumstances and find the resilience within to navigate through the challenges.

In the depths of my sorrow, I discovered the seeds of acceptance, and they blossomed into a profound sense of liberation. Acceptance became the foundation upon which I rebuilt my life, fueled with renewed purpose and a profound appreciation for the beauty that exists even in the face of adversity.

To my readers, may my story serve as a testament to the transformative power of acceptance. It is a journey that may begin in the shadows of sadness and loss, but it has the capacity to lead you toward the radiant light of triumph and a life filled with profound meaning. Embrace acceptance, for within it lies the key to unlocking the door to a future filled with resilience, joy, and a sense of self-worth.

HOW DID OBTAINING ACCEPTANCE LEAD ME TO MY NEXT STEP?

Embracing self-acceptance became the focus for my next step in life, finding happiness. This newfound happiness propelled me to shift my focus from dwelling on my weaknesses to celebrating my strengths, nurturing a wellspring of self-confidence and elevated self-esteem. Moreover, happiness allowed me to extend the same acceptance to others, encouraging them to embrace their own imperfections and fostering a profound journey of self-discovery. As anxiety and stress diminished, the weight of societal and personal expectations lifted, enabling me to breathe freely and embrace life's boundless possibilities. The ripple effects of self-acceptance echoed in my relationships as the magnetic power of positivity and support drew kindred spirits into my orbit, enriching my existence with meaningful connections. In the tapestry of life, acceptance threads joy, fulfillment, and the promise of a brighter tomorrow.

CHAPTER 5: HAPPINESS

SOME ENCOURAGING WORDS TO MY READERS:

Take the next step on the path to happiness by embracing the simple act of smiling, radiating warmth and positivity. Take the next step to happiness by fully immersing yourself in the richness of life, cherishing each moment as an opportunity for growth and fulfillment. Find happiness in the sheer miracle of existence, savoring the gift of being alive. Take the next step to happiness by cultivating financial freedom, empowering yourself to live a life of abundance and possibility. Take the next steps toward happiness by prioritizing your health, treating your body as a sacred temple and investing in your well-being. Fill your heart with boundless love and genuine appreciation for every soul in the world, embracing unity and compassion. Take the next step toward happiness by extending a helping hand to those less fortunate, experiencing the profound joy that comes from making a difference. Embrace positivity as your guiding light, taking deliberate steps toward a brighter outlook on life. And remember, happiness is contagious, so as you embark on this journey, you'll inspire others to find their own path to joy.

WHAT IS HAPPINESS?

Happiness is a subjective and multifaceted emotion that is often associated with feelings of joy, contentment, and fulfillment. It is a positive state of well-being that can be influenced by various factors, such as personal experiences, relationships, accomplishments, and one's overall outlook on life. Happiness can be found in simple pleasures, meaningful connections, pursuing passions, and experiencing a sense of purpose and meaning. It can vary from person to person, as what brings happiness to one individual may not necessarily bring the same level of happiness to another. Ultimately, happiness is a deeply personal and individual experience.

HOW OBTAINING HAPPINESS CAN BENEFIT ANYONE?

By pursuing your happiness, you are investing in your own personal growth and development, which can lead to a more fulfilling and successful life. Finding happiness can improve a person's quality of life by reducing stress, improving mental health, increasing satisfaction, and promoting overall well-being. People who are happy tend to have better relationships, more fulfilling careers, and better physical health.

Happiness can lead a person to freedom and fulfillment because it allows them to focus on what truly matters to them. When someone is happy, they are more likely to feel confident, motivated, and energized. This can lead to a greater sense of self-awareness and purpose, helping them make choices that align with their values and goals. Additionally, happiness can help individuals cultivate positive relationships and social connections, which can further enhance their sense of freedom and fulfillment. Overall, happiness can help individuals feel empowered, engaged, and fulfilled in their lives.

MY LIFE EXPERIENCE:

Now that I have embraced acceptance in my life, a beautiful transformation has unfolded, paving the way for me to pursue my ultimate happiness. It was a turning point, a pivotal moment when I discovered acceptance, and from there, I embarked on a remarkable journey to find joy and fulfillment. I wholeheartedly pursued the activities and experiences that brought me the greatest delight. I nurtured my body and mind by adopting a healthier lifestyle and delving into the world of herbs, unlocking a newfound vitality and well-being. Laughter and smiles once again became my companions, liberating me from the weight of years gone by.

As I pursued my happiness, a revelation emerged—I discovered my passion and purpose in life. I realized the immense joy that came from expressing myself through writing, entrepreneurship, and the pursuit of knowledge. Engaging in self-education became a source of empowerment, unveiling new dimensions of my capabilities that I never thought possible. The pieces of my life started to fall into place, and organization became a natural extension of my newfound happiness. With each step forward, I grew more confident in my desires and aspirations, knowing deep within that I deserved the abundant blessings that awaited me.

I gradually shed the shackles of anxiety and fear that once hindered my interactions with others. Opening up became second nature as I embraced the beauty of human connection and discovered the warmth that comes from genuine relationships. Pursuing happiness breathed life into my spirit, rekindling the fire within me. It illuminated the path that led to self-realization and allowed me to comprehend the intrinsic worth of my existence. I realized that I had been spared for a purpose—to fulfill my divine calling on this earth.

Now, a spark has been ignited within me, radiating its brilliance throughout every aspect of my being. The pursuit of happiness has become my guiding light, illuminating my way forward. It has granted me a profound understanding that my life is not only worth living but also worth cherishing and embracing wholeheartedly. I am filled with gratitude for the journey that has brought me to this moment, and I am determined to seize every opportunity, to make a positive impact, and to spread the light of happiness to all those whose paths I cross.

In finding acceptance and pursuing happiness, I have discovered the true essence of my existence—a life infused with purpose, joy, and limitless possibilities. My story continues to unfold, and with each new chapter, I embrace the magnificence of my journey, guided by the power of happiness within me.

HOW DID FINDING HAPPINESS LEAD ME TO MY NEXT STEP OF HAVING FREEDOM?

Finding happiness is a transformative journey that propels us toward experiencing true freedom in life. Cultivating happiness within ourselves unlocks the doors to liberation, freeing us from negativity, self-doubt, and societal expectations. It aligns us with our values, enabling us to pursue joy and fulfillment while liberating us from external attachments. Happiness grants us clarity, empowering us to make conscious choices that lead to a life of purpose and meaning. Ultimately, happiness serves as a stepping stone for our liberation, unlocking the boundless freedom that resides within us and revealing our true essence.

CHAPTER 6: TAKING THE NEXT STEP TO HAVING FREEDOM IN LIFE

SOME ENCOURAGING WORDS TO THE READER:

Freedom and life are not mere steps; they are the keys that unlock the door to the divine within you! No matter who you are, you possess enough to take that next step. It's the step that leads you to success, financial liberation, and freedom from depression. It's the step that ushers in prosperity, deepens your connection with God, and propels you toward personal growth and self-fulfillment. This step uncovers your passions and liberates you from the shackles of doubt and fear. Embrace this next step toward a life of freedom! In this journey, you hold the power to initiate anything, driven by faith, courage, acceptance, and happiness. Within you lies the potential to create the life you've always desired. Take the next step toward freedom, and become the best version of yourself. Seize the opportunity to share your boundless potential with the world!

WHAT IS HAVING FREEDOM IN LIFE?

Freedom is important to all life because it allows individuals to make choices and act according to their own will without being oppressed or controlled by external forces. This includes the freedom to express oneself, pursue personal goals, and live a life of dignity and fulfillment. Without freedom, individuals are unable to fully realize their potential, and society as a whole is limited in its ability to progress and innovate.

Having freedom in life is a profound state of being that allows us to experience life with expansiveness and authenticity. True freedom is the recognition that we are not confined by societal expectations or external limitations. It is the understanding that our essence is boundless, rooted in pure consciousness.

Freedom in life means fully embracing the present moment, unburdened by past regrets or future anxieties. It is a deep state of presence where we engage with life wholeheartedly and welcome its diverse experiences. It involves awakening to our eternal essence and aligning our actions with the wisdom of our higher selves. Freedom in life is living in harmony with the flow of existence, acknowledging our interconnectedness, and embracing our inherent divinity.

It is the embodiment of love, compassion, and self-acceptance, extending to others as well. We recognize ourselves as integral parts of the cosmic universe, with our unique expression contributing to the unfolding of the universe. This journey of self-discovery, self-realization, and self-transcendence leads to the liberation of our souls and the realization of oneness with all that is. Having freedom in life is an invitation to explore the depths of our being and embrace the vastness of our existence.

HOW CAN HAVING FREEDOM IN LIFE BENEFIT ANYONE?

Having freedom in your life can benefit anyone in numerous ways, enriching their overall well-being and personal growth. First, it provides a profound sense of purpose, anchoring individuals in a direction that aligns with their authentic selves. When one embraces freedom, they are empowered to make choices that resonate with their deepest values and aspirations, creating a life that feels meaningful and fulfilling.

Having freedom brings forth self-confidence and self-esteem. By taking decisive steps toward their goals and aspirations, individuals develop a belief in their own abilities and worth. They recognize that they have the power to shape their own destiny, which bolsters their confidence in facing challenges and seizing opportunities with courage and resilience.

The pursuit of freedom leads to an expanded repetition of experiences and skills. As individuals take action toward their aspirations, they open themselves to new possibilities and learn along the way. This journey of growth and self-discovery enhances their personal and professional development, equipping them with valuable insights, expertise, and adaptability.

Having freedom in life also brings forth immense joy and excitement. When individuals actively pursue their passions and interests, they tap into a wellspring of enthusiasm and fulfillment. Engaging in activities that truly resonate with their hearts and souls allows them to experience a profound sense of fulfillment and satisfaction, infusing every moment with purpose.

By taking the next steps toward life and freedom, individuals embark on a journey of self-discovery, empowerment, and the creation of a more satisfying and rewarding existence.

MY LIFE EXPERIENCE:

Let me share with you this continuously powerful chapter of my life, where I triumphed over overwhelming obstacles and embraced the true meaning of freedom. In this moment, as I reflect on my journey, I stand tall in faith, courage, acceptance, happiness, and the profound freedom that courses through my veins.

I have reached a place of acceptance where my wheelchair is no longer a symbol of limitation but a faithful companion that propels me forward. Chains of depression, insecurities, and a lack of courage have been shattered, never to hold me captive again. Every day, I am blessed to be a part of this magnificent world, cherishing the gift of my existence.

Now, I understand the interconnection between all living beings, recognizing the profound unity that binds us all together. My passion and purpose for the world have become clear, illuminating my path with unflinching determination. I know why I am here, and my very existence bears testament to the strength of the human spirit.

The journey from where I started was confusing and heartbreaking, draining me emotionally, physically, and spiritually. Yet, I rose above the challenges, overcoming the unexpected changes and pitfalls that threatened to consume me. Today, I stand as a testament to resilience, a living embodiment of triumph over adversity.

I have transformed into a better version of myself, continuously taking small steps toward becoming the best version of myself that I can be. The fact that I am actively writing this book with the intent of inspiring and uplifting others fills my heart with grace and gratitude. From a place of immobility, I now walk with the power of my words, knowing that this is the divine will guiding my purposeful journey.

My life experiences are a testament to the human spirit's enduring strength and the power of faith. They serve as a beacon of hope for those facing overwhelming obstacles, reminding them that freedom is attainable, even in the face of adversity. Embrace your challenges, for they are the stepping stones that lead to your true liberation. Trust in the unfolding of your own magnificent story, and let the world witness the triumphant power that lies within you.

CHAPTER 7: INTERVIEWS

These interviews with random individuals hold a profound purpose: to remind us that each person's journey in life is unique and that we are never alone in our struggles and fears. Often, we mistakenly believe that our suffering is exclusive and that the world revolves around us. We judge situations with bias, failing to recognize the universality of human experiences. It is crucial to understand the origins of suffering in order to overcome it and empower ourselves to take the next step toward growth and liberation.

During these interviews, the focus was not on the interviewee's name, race, or age, but rather on two fundamental questions: How they would describe themselves and whether there was a significant change or pivotal moment that compelled them to embark on their next step in life. These questions aimed to delve into their personal reflections, revealing insights into their self-perception and the transformative experiences that ignited their journey forward.

INTERVIEWEE 1: HOW WOULD YOU DESCRIBE YOURSELF?

I am a proud man who embodies multiple roles in life. I am a devoted son and brother, bringing love and support to my family. As an uncle, I cherish the opportunity to be a positive influence in the lives of my nieces and nephews. Professionally, I hold the title of a master business administrator, utilizing my intelligence and expertise to navigate the corporate world.

On a personal level, I am characterized by qualities of love, care, and helpfulness, always striving to lend a helping hand and make a positive impact. I am thoughtful in my actions, considering the well-being of others. Determination fuels my pursuits, driving me to achieve my goals and overcome challenges. At times, I can be stubborn, but I recognize the need for flexibility and growth. And while I acknowledge occasional moments of self-interest, I aspire to balance my entrepreneurial ambitions with compassion and selflessness.

WHAT WAS THE SIGNIFICANT CHANGE OR PIVOTAL MOMENT THAT COMPELLED YOU TO EMBARK ON YOUR NEXT STEP IN LIFE?

In 2016, I experienced a series of devastating setbacks that stripped away everything I had worked for. I lost my job, my career status, and found myself facing unemployment. The comfortable life I had built was suddenly shattered, forcing me to downsize and share an apartment with a roommate. Eventually, I had no choice but to return home, feeling defeated and consumed by depression. It was a moment of profound brokenness, one where I questioned my purpose and my worth.

But in the midst of this despair, I realized that this pivotal moment held the potential for transformation. It became clear to me that my next step in life was not just about finding a new job or rebuilding my external circumstances. It was about embarking on a journey of inner growth and rediscovery.

I recognized that the first step on this path was to rebuild my faith, not only in a higher power but also in myself. I had to dig deep and find the strength to believe in my own resilience and potential. It was a challenging process that required me to confront my past, accept my present reality, and let go of the weight of my failures.

Through this process of self-reflection and self-acceptance, I began to find happiness and contentment in the present moment. I learned to release the grip of the past and embrace the person I had become. It was a second chance to build a life rooted in self-love and appreciation.

While the journey was not easy, it was necessary for my growth and personal development. It taught me the value of resilience, perseverance, and the power of the human spirit. Today, I am grateful for the lessons I learned during that challenging time, as they have shaped me into a stronger and more compassionate individual.

This significant change compelled me to embark on a profound transformation, one that goes beyond external achievements. It awakened a deeper understanding of my own worth and the importance of finding happiness within myself. It sparked a journey of self-discovery and personal fulfillment as I embraced the next step of rebuilding my life from the inside out.

INTERVIEWEE 2: HOW WOULD YOU DESCRIBE YOURSELF?

I am a woman, happily married and blessed with four beautiful children. My profession as a teacher and educator allows me to make a positive impact on young minds and shape the future generation. I am described as a person with a kind and gentle heart, guided by my faith and fear of God. With a good sense of humor, I believe in bringing joy and laughter into the lives of those around me. I approach life with an open mind, eager to learn and grow. One of my greatest strengths is my ability to show compassion and empathy toward others, recognizing the importance of understanding and supporting one another.

WHAT WAS THE SIGNIFICANT CHANGE OR PIVOTAL MOMENT THAT COMPELLED YOU TO EMBARK ON YOUR NEXT STEP IN LIFE?

The pivotal moment that compelled me to embark on my next step in life was when I welcomed my first child into the world. It was a profound realization that life was no longer solely about me; it ignited a deep sense of responsibility and purpose. Prior to becoming a mother, I had been navigating through life without a clear direction, lacking motivation, and thinking I had all the time in the world. However, my daughter's arrival made me understand the importance of taking life seriously and growing as an individual.

Another significant turning point occurred with the birth of my second child, my son. This inspired me to prioritize my health and financial stability, ensuring that I could provide for my children's well-being. By taking those steps toward self-improvement, I experienced personal growth and stability. I pursued my dream job as a special education teacher, obtaining my master's degree and finding fulfillment in making a positive impact on the lives of others.

Yet another pivotal moment arose years later, following the birth of my last child. I realized that I had become disconnected from my faith and was merely going through the motions of life. My job had lost its spark, and everything felt like a repetitive routine. Determined to break free from this cycle, I sought to create a life filled with meaningful moments. I began to reevaluate myself, my priorities, and the importance of self-care. I reconnected with my faith, resulting in a renewed sense of joy, increased confidence, and greater ease in navigating life's challenges.

Each step I took in life brought about positive transformations, molding me into a better version of myself. The journey of motherhood and the pursuit of personal growth have taught me the value of responsibility, self-reflection, and finding balance. I now embrace life with a brighter smile, increased confidence, and a deeper appreciation for the moments that shape my story.

INTERVIEWEE 3: HOW WOULD YOU DESCRIBE YOURSELF?

I am a resilient man who wears multiple hats in life. I am a devoted husband and a loving father to my precious child, cherishing the joys and responsibilities that come with these roles. As an entrepreneur, I embark on ventures that allow me to express my creativity and strive for success. My educational journey has led me to graduate from college, and I am now pursuing a master's degree to fulfill my aspiration of becoming a Clinical Mental Health counselor, driven by my unwavering passion for helping others navigate their emotional well-being.

In reflecting on my life experiences, I acknowledge the sins of my past. I have confronted the darkness of my earlier days as a former drug dealer, channeling those experiences into lessons that have shaped me into the person I am today. With a thirst for exploration, I embrace the world as a traveler, immersing myself in different cultures and discovering the beauty of diversity. With an outgoing nature, I seek connection and meaningful interactions, appreciating the power of human connection.

WHAT WAS THE SIGNIFICANT CHANGE OR PIVOTAL MOMENT THAT COMPELLED YOU TO EMBARK ON YOUR NEXT STEP IN LIFE?

The pivotal moment that reshaped my life's journey was my time spent in prison. Though seemingly a dark and challenging period, it proved to be a transformative experience that propelled me forward. Behind those prison walls, I was granted the gift of emptiness and self-reflection. It was there that I confronted my past mistakes head-on and embraced the opportunity to learn from them.

Within the confines of those walls, a revelation dawned upon me. I realized that my mind, my God-giving gift, held immense power to make a positive impact on the lives of others. As I envisioned the day of my release, I made a solemn promise to myself: I would utilize my newfound wisdom and empathy to uplift and support individuals in need.

Stepping out of those prison gates, a world of possibilities awaited me. Armed with resilience, determination, and a deep desire to help others, I embarked on a journey toward mental health advocacy, particularly focusing on the well-being of young and older people of color. Through my own lived experiences, I am uniquely equipped to empathize, understand, and guide those who may be facing similar challenges.
This next step in my life has opened countless doors and presented me with remarkable opportunities. I now stand poised to make a difference, to break down barriers, and to inspire individuals to embrace their own

transformative journeys. With every interaction, I aim to instill hope, ignite resilience, and empower others to rewrite their own narratives.

Looking ahead, I am fueled by a sense of purpose and a fervent belief in the human capacity for growth and redemption. I am driven to create a world where mental health is prioritized, where compassion and understanding thrive, and where every individual, regardless of their past, has the opportunity to rise and thrive.

INTERVIEWEE 4: HOW WOULD YOU DESCRIBE YOURSELF?

I describe myself as a determined woman, standing tall and resolute. As a fearless goal-getter, I pursue my ambitions with focus and purpose. I proudly embrace the roles of a loving daughter and a dedicated mother, providing strength to my two precious children despite the challenges I've faced, including the loss of my partner.

Beyond motherhood, I am an accomplished artist and skilled graphics illustration designer, bringing various designs to life with an unwavering commitment to excellence. With a degree in art and culture, I find genuine satisfaction in my craft and approach life with a heartfelt smile.

In all aspects of my life, I seize my opportunities wisely, firmly believing in the power of positivity and embracing the endless possibilities that come my way.

WHAT WAS THE SIGNIFICANT CHANGE OR PIVOTAL MOMENT THAT COMPELLED YOU TO EMBARK ON YOUR NEXT STEP IN LIFE?

The significant change or pivotal moment that compelled me to embark on my next step in life was the heartbreaking loss of my beloved husband. This devastating event brought forth a powerful realization that I needed to gather all my strength to ensure I would not fail my children. I foresaw the challenges and the standards that lay ahead, and it became my driving force to rise up even stronger.

With the responsibilities of providing a secure and comfortable life for my family weighing on my mind, I understood that I had different stages of life to navigate and conquer. Visualizing a future filled with beauty and progress, I felt a deep determination to reach that better stage as soon as possible.

I recognized that bridges are meant to be climbed, and I embraced the satisfaction that comes from overcoming obstacles and reaching a place of tranquility. In this defining moment, I realized the importance of faith and acceptance, as they became essential pillars of strength for me and my two boys. Though the situation I faced was unexpected, I summoned the courage and resilience necessary to push forward and overcome the challenges that lay before me.

INTERVIEWEE 5: HOW WOULD YOU DESCRIBE YOURSELF?

I'm a man, a devoted single father, and a supportive brother. My character can be best described as humble and modest, grounded in a down-to-earth nature that keeps me connected to others. I'm very ambitious— determined to continuously improve myself. I am fueled by a strong work ethic and unwavering dedication to my goals. With focus, I strive to make every moment count and seize opportunities that come my way.

WHAT WAS THE SIGNIFICANT CHANGE OR PIVOTAL MOMENT THAT COMPELLED YOU TO EMBARK ON YOUR NEXT STEP IN LIFE?

In my childhood struggles, around the tender age of 12, I encountered a pivotal moment that would shape the course of my life. Growing up without a male role model and facing financial hardships, my family and I struggled to make ends meet. I yearned to bring happiness to my loved ones, to uplift them from the burdens we carried. In a single-parent household, the absence of my father weighed heavily on my mind, forcing me to mature beyond my years.

Driven by the desire to support my mother, I took on various responsibilities at a young age. From tending to the yard to assisting my uncles and even delving into construction work, I absorbed the value of hard work. This early exposure to labor instilled in me a profound understanding of the importance of perseverance and dedication.

Since those formative years, my pursuit of happiness has been unwavering. I have been relentlessly chasing the keys to living a fulfilling and prosperous life. Every step I take is fueled by the determination to overcome obstacles and create a better future for myself and my family. Through resilience and an unwavering spirit, I am charting my path toward a life filled with joy, success, and the fulfillment of my deepest aspirations.

INTERVIEWEE 6: HOW WOULD YOU DESCRIBE YOURSELF?

I am a woman who unapologetically embraces her unique qualities. Within the depths of my being, I carry a captivating blend of introversion and geekiness, finding solace and inspiration in the pages of comic books. My thirst for knowledge knows no bounds, as I wholeheartedly embrace the power of education, recognizing it as both a strength and a catalyst for personal growth. With a brilliant mind as my ally, I navigate life's challenges with ease and grace.

I radiate warmth and kindness, extending a welcoming embrace to all who cross my path. As a devoted wife, I foster love and connection in the sacred bond of marriage. My determination fuels my career aspirations, propelling me toward success and fulfillment. I am driven by a deep sense of purpose, dedicating myself wholeheartedly to my chosen path. In essence, I am a compassionate soul and an unstoppable force of ambition.

WHAT WAS THE SIGNIFICANT CHANGE OR PIVOTAL MOMENT THAT COMPELLED YOU TO EMBARK ON YOUR NEXT STEP IN LIFE?

The significant change that compelled me to embark on my next step in life came with a profound loss. In the depths of grief and darkness after losing a child, I felt like I had lost a part of myself. It was a period of immense pain and confusion as I struggled to navigate the overwhelming emotions and find a way to heal.

During this challenging time, my faith was put to the test. I questioned everything, including myself and my purpose. I couldn't comprehend why such a heartbreaking event had occurred in my life. It was a moment of deep introspection and self-doubt.

However, I recognized the need to reinvent myself and start anew. I realized that in order to truly live again, a part of me had to let go and transform. It was a journey of self-discovery and personal growth, where I sought to find my own path and redefine my identity.

This pivotal moment compelled me to seek healing and inner strength. I embarked on a journey of self-reflection and self-empowerment, embracing the lessons learned from my pain and using them as catalysts for personal transformation. Through faith, acceptance, and belief in my own capacity to grow, I embarked on a new chapter of my life, determined to become a better version of myself.

INTERVIEWEE 7: HOW WOULD YOU DESCRIBE YOURSELF?

I am a man. As a father of 7 wonderful kids, I strive to be honest and dedicated in all that I do. My determination and focus drive me toward achieving my life goals. I have an easygoing nature and cherish my roles as a son, husband, brother, and uncle. Spending quality time with my kids brings me immense joy, and I prioritize my family above all else. I am happily married and value the importance of family bonds.

WHAT WAS THE SIGNIFICANT CHANGE OR PIVOTAL MOMENT THAT COMPELLED YOU TO EMBARK ON YOUR NEXT STEP IN LIFE?

The pivotal moment that propelled me toward my next step in life was the day I entered into marriage in 2015. It sparked a series of transformative changes and inspired me to strive for a better future. In order to support my growing family, I actively sought new employment opportunities, leaving behind the life of a single parent with a child. This marked the beginning of a journey toward a brighter existence. Simultaneously, my marriage served as a stepping stone toward strengthening my faith. I was determined to make my marriage thrive, constantly learning how to be a better husband and provider. As the father of the household, I realized the weight of the responsibilities placed upon me. However, through faith, I discovered the courage to embrace the challenges. I understood that marriage is a lifetime voyage, one that requires continuous effort and dedication. With faith as my guide, I learned to fearlessly work at building a harmonious, fulfilling, and beautiful family life at all times.

INTERVIEWEE 8: HOW WOULD YOU DESCRIBE YOURSELF?

I am a radiant woman, proudly embracing the roles that life has cast upon me. I am a mother of three, and I find fulfillment in nurturing their growth and guiding them on their journeys. As a Gemini, I embody the duality of strength and adaptability, harnessing these qualities to navigate life's twists and turns. I am a loving daughter, cherishing the bond with my own parents. Being an auntie brings me great joy as I watch my nieces and nephews grow into their own unique selves. With determination and ambition, I pursue my dreams and strive for success. I am also blessed to embrace the precious title of grandmother, witnessing the beauty of life's circle unfolding before my eyes. Overall, I am a multifaceted individual, radiating happiness and embracing the richness of the roles I play in this grand tapestry of life.

WHAT WAS THE SIGNIFICANT CHANGE OR PIVOTAL MOMENT THAT COMPELLED YOU TO EMBARK ON YOUR NEXT STEP IN LIFE?

The moment I walked away from my marriage, I embarked on a transformative journey of self-discovery and empowerment. It was a pivotal moment that compelled me to embrace faith and independence as my guiding lights. Suddenly, I found myself shouldering new responsibilities and facing the importance of financial stability. The dream of being taken care of and having a blissful marriage was no more, but in its absence, I discovered my own strength. Despite the challenges, I boldly assumed the roles of both parents, taking charge of my life and paying all the bills with unwavering determination. This significant change ignited a fire within me to create a life of resilience, purpose, and fulfillment.

INTERVIEWEE 9:HOW WOULD YOU DESCRIBE YOURSELF?

I'm a man, and I proudly embrace the role of a loving father to my four amazing children. I am a compassionate and understanding individual, always ready to lend a helping hand. As a brother, son, and uncle, I cherish the bonds of family and strive to be a positive influence in their lives. Furthermore, I am committed to personal growth and constantly working toward becoming the best version of myself.

WHAT WAS THE SIGNIFICANT CHANGE OR PIVOTAL MOMENT THAT COMPELLED YOU TO EMBARK ON YOUR NEXT STEP IN LIFE?

The significant change that compelled me to embark on my next step in life was a pivotal moment when I realized the detrimental effects of neglecting my health and well-being. I reached a turning point where I witnessed my health deteriorating, my mood shifting, and my ability to concentrate diminishing. It was a wake-up call that urged me to take a step of faith toward transformation. Although I occasionally stumble off track and face challenges, I acknowledge my weaknesses and commit to reforming myself. I am determined to reestablish a balanced and nourishing diet, cultivate discipline and focus, and incorporate consistent meditation practices. With consistency and determination, I am driven to become a better version of myself, embracing a healthier and more fulfilling life journey.

INTERVIEWEE 10: HOW WOULD YOU DESCRIBE YOURSELF?

I am a vibrant woman, radiating positivity and inspiration. As a helpful and supportive friend, I am always there to lift others up. Embracing motherhood with grace, I nurture and guide five beautiful souls. My talents shine brightly, igniting passion in all that I do. While I may have moments of strength, I strive to be kind and compassionate, always considering others' needs. My journey is one of growth, evolving into the best version of myself.

WHAT WAS THE SIGNIFICANT CHANGE OR PIVOTAL MOMENT THAT COMPELLED YOU TO EMBARK ON YOUR NEXT STEP IN LIFE?

The pivotal moment that compelled me to embark on my next step in life was when I faced the darkness of abuse and fought a seemingly uphill battle. Lost in the streets, feeling isolated and alone, I yearned to understand and connect with others, but it seemed like an impossible task. However, through this challenging journey, I discovered the power of faith, acceptance, and courage. With faith, I found the strength to move forward. Embracing acceptance allowed me to release the weight of the past and embrace the present. With courage, I left the shadows behind and stepped boldly into a new chapter of my life.

Today, I stand tall and proud of the person I have become. My journey has granted me the gift of sharing my story, inspiring others to find their own strength and resilience. I am a symbol of hope and empowerment, using my experiences to encourage others on their path to healing and transformation. Embracing my truth has set me free, and I now walk with purpose and determination, knowing that my story can inspire and uplift others. I cherish the blessing of being able to uplift and support those who have faced similar challenges, guiding them toward their own triumphs.

Rewrite the pivotal moments in your life down and reflect on how you took the next step forward to overcome your situation! This exercise helps you to learn from the past and rediscover what you were able to overcome.

CHAPTER 8: POEMS AND AFFIRMATIONS

PORTRAYER

The Portrayer, a symbol of what you falsely aspire to be, chasing societal norms while forsaking your authenticity.

They paint a picture of fame, wealth, and materialistic spree While concealing their essence within the lost identity.

Confidence and joy radiate from their exterior display; Yet, deep inside, cries of loneliness and disparity lead the way.

In their righteousness, they believe no wrong can be, But failure looms as they refuse to alter the tune of their melody.

Blinded by optimism, they believe all will align, Ignorant that faith without work makes it impossible to shine.

They bask in comfort, stagnant in their own position, Ill-informed to the fact that growth grants freedom, a transformative mission.

They influence many, preaching how life is all good,

But fail to live their words, decaying progress like rotting wood.

Deep inside, the Portrayer doubts their own self-worth;
Yet that same energy could unveil the God within to birth.

They drain your spirit, consuming your vital energy,
Steering you further from your path, delaying your destiny.

So let us break free from the Portrayer's snare,
And embrace our true selves, for the greatness within we declare.

As we learn from the famous Portrayer's tale,
To seek authenticity and true success, the Portrayer must fail!

EMOTIONALLY HUMANE

Emotionally Humane is the treasure lost throughout creation. The missing link to Unity, completing the equation.

Emotionally Humane is the melody to perfect harmony,
Synchronizing the love in hearts, in all of humanity.

Inspiring unity, like standing trees connecting roots
Living together beneath the starful sky because we share the same roof.

In this cosmic dance, we share existence together,

an evolution of courage when love binds us together.

Hatred we banish, replacing it with peace's face.
A world where happiness runs wild in its rightful place.

Acceptance begins blooming like spring flowers,
While forgiveness only takes seconds, no more hours.

Racism dismantled, its power defeated,
No unjust liberty, but equality completed.

See yourself in others, their joys and their fears, For we're
bound by humanity, universal peers.

Compassion is now like the wind, uncontrollable flow.
We're all threads of perfection, so let our beauty glow.

Powerful golden sun rays are our radiant freedom's light.
Shattering illusions, crumbling walls, forging of a new
world in sight.

Within us, life's tools are gifted. Within our reach, they lie.
But growth takes time, like the nurturing of a child, until
they rise.

With faith, cultivate the God within,
For greatness unfolds in us all as we rise and begin.

Emotionally Humane should be in our collective
thoughts,
While heaven on earth should be the symphony echoing
in our hearts.

A call to action, transforming space and time. This is Emotionally Humane for the Enlightened Mind!

AFFIRMATIONS:

These affirmations, carefully crafted from experiences of my own journey, are now shared with my readers with the intention of inspiring, empowering, and offering assistance to anyone who embraces them.

1. Nobody can make anybody change, but everybody has the power to change!
2. The projection of one's self is always different when viewed through a different eye!
3. Your purpose in life is to find your purpose for life!
4. Always remember, it's your dream, and it dies if you give up!
5. Changed the world one place at a time.
6. He who lives in the hearts of the people lives forever.
7. Appreciate yourself in the present moment.
8. We were predestined to evolve and elevate.
9. I embrace my authentic self and recognize that I am somebody extraordinary.
10. I see a reflection of myself in every person I encounter, extending compassion, support, and nourishment to those in need.
11. I emulate the essence of heaven as I navigate the world with divine purpose.
12. By conquering my fears and doubts, I unlock the gates to my true greatness.

13. My words carry the power to inspire and uplift, so I choose them wisely and speak with intention.
14. The more I give, the more abundance flows into my life. Taking without giving leaves me empty-handed.
15. Success is not dependent on others' support, but on my deep belief in myself, which attracts the support I need.
16. Sometimes the simplest path can lead one to the clearest destination.
17. When I awaken the divine presence within me, I am able to experience the beauty of heaven here on earth.
18. Divine ideas can only create togetherness!
19. God's spirit, love, and essence pour through me!

Whatever your next step is, make sure it's a step toward your own greatness!

 Use what you already possess to unlock all that's within!

"Out of difficulties grow miracles." – Jean de La Bruyere

The Will of God Resides Within Us All!

The End